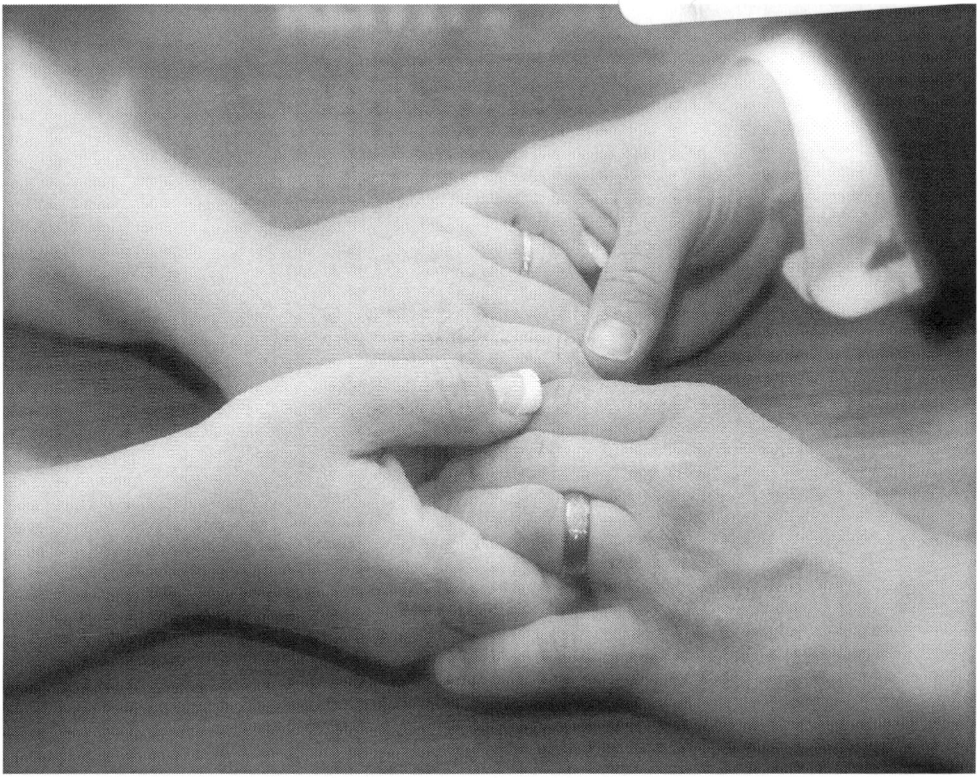

THE A, B, C,'S
OF MARRIAGE

COPYRIGHT

MARRIAGE TIPS
AND
WORKSHEETS

WISDOM GAINED
FROM THE LETTER

A

BOOK 2

BY
MARLENE BIERWORTH

DEDICATION

I am writing this book series for all those who have walked down the isle only to find that the walk through life is proving to be much more difficult.

The desire for marital success,

to be 'the best we can be'

together and forever

is the foremost seed that you will need to succeed. I trust that the tiny seed you planted on your wedding day will take hold, grow and blossom to it's full potential, both individually and as a couple. I trust that as a couple you will debate the **ABC'S of Marriage** and apply the information to the places that need changed or improved. I trust that even if you are taking the first steps of change alone, without your partner's support, that you will stand firm and believe that he or she will come alongside, as you do your part.

Lastly, I would like to thank my husband, Paul, for the love and commitment that I have enjoyed for the past

43 years. Never a day has gone by that we have not uttered those three powerful words, "I love you", and lived them out in some random act of selfless giving. That is our secret and part of my authority in sharing these thoughts with you. I gain knowledge from life, trial and error, council and research. I gain wisdom from the bible for it is the foundation of marriage and the heart of relationship. I gain victory from the application of truth to my daily life and a partner who loves unconditionally, in the good times and bad.

The book has been written with study and work exercises you can do together as a couple, or alone, as you pave the way to a personal success that will in turn trigger marital success.

We are continuing with the letter A and moving along in subsequent books in the series. I have featured 5 titles in each section, 3 sections in each book that will call you to action. **You set your own pace**! If you need to linger longer on one truth, stay there until it has been fully analyzed, written on your hearts and practiced in your everyday responses to one another. **It is not a race against fellow competitors! Better to run your race and finish well!** If the first section takes you a month, celebrate that, for the truth will have taken root in you as individuals and into the very foundation of your marriage. The disciplined results have the power to last for a lifetime.

Remember, individual strength and stability are the necessary components to success as a couple!

PREFACE

Marriage is a well-covered subject in this age of bountiful knowledge. Yet, **knowledge without application is useless**. If you have not come to grips with that extremely important fact, then more information will not help to alter your understanding of the mysteries of marriage. Facts lead to understanding, then to application, and finally finish with our ultimate goal: a changed life (personally), and a changed marriage (as a couple).

You can devour volumes of information, be legitimately hungry for change, have all the marriage-tips at your fingertips, and still not succeed.

There are questions you need to ask yourself at the onset of this marriage challenge:
Are you willing to apply the truth to your situation?
Are you willing to take the lead to redeem your marriage?

Are you willing to be patient with your not-so-cooperative mate?

Are you willing to be diligent in the process?

Are you willing to put aside any pre-set ideas and consider new ones?

Are you willing to take ownership of the problems and solutions?

If you are reading this as a couple, I commend you. The very fact that you are both open to knowledge, wisdom, character study, and the challenge of application in many of your life situations, sets you on a sure path to victory.

Claim it right now!

Decide that you will grow deeper in relationship.

Decide that you will listen to your partner's needs.

Decide that you will apply truth to your side of the problem.

Decide that you will remember manners and decency.

Decide that you will try to out-give your partner.

Decide that you will remain faithful to your wedding vows.

Decide that you will safeguard emotional and privacy issues.

Marriage can be the ultimate relationship experience!

I am sure that was the intention from the beginning. No one enters matrimony with the conscious, sole determination to fail, but many succumb to it because it's just too hard! But, hard work has a payday.

A great life is the benefit of a great marriage.
So, let's get to work! Are you ready for payday?
The first 3 sections of titles are in Book 1.
This book starts with Section 4

A

ALPHA

ALWAYS

AMAZE

AMBITION

AMEND

16. ALPHA

Alpha is the first letter of the Greek alphabet. Those of us who are Christians relate to this word for it is a word attributed to God. He is the first but He is also the last, 'Omega' being the last

Can you relate to this definition within the perimeters of your marriage? Is your spouse your first and your last? Of course we all know there are unwelcomed exceptions to this commitment. Adulthood is a long time and unplanned and unexpected events set new borders for the best-laid commitments. Death, abuse, fornication and unfortunately divorce are the major four.

Realistically, there will be times when the first spouse will not be the last. But once again I want to reinforce the concept I stated earlier that decisions to terminate our present marital status needs to be based on issues that are beyond your control to fix and not just an excuse for escape to a self-imagined greener pasture.

I believe that you are committed to making it work with your current spouse otherwise you would not be actively seeking marriage counsel that could bring healing and help to your scarred relationships.

For others you have realized that marriage is a 24/7 training ground and are open to all tips and challenges to keep it running smoothly or create some new sparks to enhance a forever growing and changing relationship.

I also dare to believe that a man can still desire to grow old with the bride of his youth, and the woman can still set goals for the Cinderella dream to love her man forever. It was with raw emotion and a meager glimpse at the idea of love that captivated us in the beginning of our relationship. Truthfully, when you now look back to that 'first love' you realize just how little you knew about the everyday struggles of living with your spouse. But, the good news is that every challenge and heartbreak can serve as fuel and used to ignite healthy personal change.

I am sure by now that you have realized you are not going to change your partner, certainly not in any way that will benefit your relationship for the long term. And you shouldn't even try. Save yourself a lot of pain and conflict by resigning yourself to simply loving them and then standing back to watch the miracle unfold. They will never grow into the person your selfish heart demands, but in response to your unconditional love they will indeed rise to the top. Together you will become everything necessary to succeed as an individual, as a couple and as a family.

Sounds easy: Certainly not! Our human ego will fight it every step of the way. But the rewards for patience in this area are well worth it. The saying, the "two shall become one" is very true when applied to a marriage relationship. Have you heard or seen older couples that actually start to resemble one another, their outward presence essentially reflecting their partner? They know one anther's responses, favorite things, values, convictions; they share intimate memories with mutual family and friends; in essence they have history together.

The question is can you erase history? No, it follows you for life. In the case of a second marriage you enter transformed for the better or the worse. This is commonly known as unwanted baggage in a new relationship and will cause double the trouble for guaranteeing any future success. Don't despair if you are already there. Baggage can be overcome but be prepared to work hard and selflessly to allow new history to develop with new people while still attempting to juggle the old into your schedule.

With that truth presently nagging your conscience, I would encourage you to work hard to resurrect your present relationship and let it be your last. The Omega victory!

The legacy and influence we leave behind, for others to witness and imitate, will stretch far into eternity. Be sure to diligently plant hope into the hearts of those you love; the hope that keeps us all fruitful from this day forward until the end of life's journey.

The Alpha and the Omega!

'ALPHA' WORKSHEET

1. Is your present spouse your 'first'?

2. If not, what were the details of separation from your 'first love'?

3. What were your expectations from Day 1 of your present marriage?

4. Does your spouse have the same dreams and hopes of you being their 'first and last'? Discuss them openly.

5. Has the walk been easy? Discuss and gain encouragement from the hurdles already conquered.

6. Do you have a plan, both individually and as a couple on how you will make it to the golden years together?

7. Do you live married life by 'the seat of your pants', being thrown into emotional exhaustion at every unexpected turn of events?

8 How can you solidify your commitment to each other in this area of longevity?

17. ALWAYS

Always is an adjective describing the many areas of life that we will be or do "at all times". Not just some of the time, when I feel like it or when it is convenient, but ALL OF THE TIME. Big commitment!

- This revelation silently demands of us to daily make good choices that will affect relationships for years to come.
- This revelation demands of us to not grow weary or bored.
- This revelation grows on the foundation of who we are and hope to be both as individuals and couples.
- This revelation requires selfless giving and unconditional love.
- This revelation will nurture security and commitment for the long haul.

When ALL OF THE TIME becomes difficult, and it will, we need to choose to ask for forgiveness, we need to choose to love 'in spite of", then regroup and move on.

What areas are we required to 'ALWAYS' be there for our spouse?

- Always be respectful
- Always be honorable
- Always be supportive
- Always respond in kindness
- Always be dependable
- Always love unconditionally
- Always place them first in your life
- Always be considerate of their feelings and fatigue
- Always when it involves character choices

And the list goes on and on. The wonderful truth is that you are only half of the relationship. When the two of you attack this list of selfless, **always behavior**, the miracle happens. The two halves become one whole and both partners are satisfied and gratified. I can't emphasize that point enough.

Always walk confidently in your marriage roles and don't try to conquer life's hard-to-climb mountains alone. Grab hold of your partner's hand and tackle the jagged rocks together. You will ultimately reach the pinnacle, perhaps scarred somewhat, but definitely together, stronger and enshrouded with new family history.

'Always' is always the right road to travel.

'ALWAYS' WORKSHEET

1. What does 'always' in the context of marriage mean to you and your partner.

2. Do you feel the idea of 'always' overwhelming and unachievable?

3. What perimeters of grace can you set for one another when conflicts arise?

4. How many times should you forgive a heart that yearns to walk in the truth of 'always' being there for their spouse, yet stumbles?

5. Does God have a finite 'mercy number' for you?

6. Can you integrate the idea of you being only 'one half of a whole' in your marriage partnership? Define that for each other.

7. Do you need to set perimeters in your lives that will protect and balance the 'whole' picture?

8. Are you both climbing the mountains of life together, growing into stronger and healthier individuals?

18. AMAZE

Most people love to be amazed. To be filled with wonder. It's the spectacular moments in life that impart hope, a proverbial bright spot in an otherwise dull and routine day. Do people have the ability to amaze you? Do you allow them this opportunity or do you shut them down upon approach? Most importantly, does your spouse still have the ability to amaze you?

I know he did at one time. It was particularly evident during the engagement period when the love of your life could do not wrong, or if they did they were quickly forgiven. Why? Because in the case of the one you love, it is a proven fact that every word spoken, every selfless deed intended for you, holds you captive. You are mesmerized by their charms and your partner has the ability to amaze you, over and over again.

Did you plan or even consider the possibility that this well cherished infatuation would ever diminish over time? Certainly not, but life, jobs, stress, family, social pressures, fatigue and compromise have somehow managed to dull the singular focus. Now we almost need to mark such moments on our calendar, unless of course you possess the gift of spontaneity or you have effectively ingrained the act of amazing your partner into your very inner being.

Our reactions, our fascination, the spontaneity, the surprise acts that held you spellbound and constantly reminded you of your love and need for your spouse, all require of us to consciously and habitually remain focused on amazing them. If we do we are going to enjoy this amazing blessing throughout our lifetime.

In essence it is important to remember, that when life hits you hard, when you are in the midst of being torn in multi-directions, when it is hard to summon any sliver of 'amazement', that is the time when you need to push harder. It's in the midst of these special moments of your day that the stresses of life takes a break; these are the moments that make you smile and push you forward with renewed vigor. Learn how to effectively dish them out and gratefully receive them.

Keep your marriage alive and well, constantly renewed with the gift of amazement. It is indeed possible to be amazed, again and still again. Brought to you by 'joy' and all designed for your 'lifetime of pleasure.'

'AMAZE' WORKSHEET

1. Does your spouse still have the ability to amaze you or have you become cold to any efforts they attempt? What do they think of your answer?

2. Do you still feel the love-tugs, the pitty-patter of the heartstrings?
If no, discuss ways you can reclaim it.

3. With all the demands of life, do you still make time for your spouse, to embrace those special moments?

4. Amazement is like the rays of 'honeymoon' on the go. Are you still there?

Perhaps you and your spouse have not given this issue a second thought lately and are settled into the humdrums of daily existence.

Take the time now. Talk of ways you can satisfy this need in each other.

19. AMBITION

Ambition has the ability to be a strong positive force in your lifetime but it can equally be a destructive quality if not kept under control. With it comes 'an *eager desire*' and there is certainly nothing wrong with that, right? 'Eager' provides motivation, great joy to do something. What you ask? The rest of the definition answers that. *For attaining honor, fame or power!*

Honor is certainly a noble characteristic and one that we should all seek diligently. To have an honorable reputation is desirous and necessary if we are to work in the kingdom of God; if we are to leave a powerful legacy to our loved ones; if we are to gain respect from our colleagues. It is a powerful positive attribute that will sew greatly into the lives of others. Be sure that in your quest to be honorable that your motives are pure and humble. People will see through a fraud. It is a select few that gain the distinction of honor. Be sure that your spouse and family are your biggest fans.

Fame is certainly a position of achievement. You've worked hard for that recognition and in itself can be a positive influence in our world. Millions listen attentively to famous people for any words of wisdom uttered from their lips or written by their hand. A famous person has a place of influence in the lives of others and with it comes great responsibility. Remember that the ultimate fame is found within the wall of your home. To gain worldly recognition but neglect your family in this area is counterproductive and will not win you any crowns in heaven. Be sure to be a hero at home and leave a famous legacy there as part of your history.

Next is power; the one you've been waiting for. It is a human tendency for man to seek power. It started in the Garden of Eden. Adam and Eve were not content to play the roles that God so graciously bestowed on them or to be obedient to the one rule that would eternally protect them from destruction. Pride and power whispered lies in their ears and said they could be like God and they bought the power trip, hook line and sinker, and sin entered the world. Power is often associated with sinful actions that hurt, demean, gloat and manipulate. The world pushes them forward, up the prideful climb of the success ladder regardless of who gets trampled.

Never go on a power trip with the ones you love. This serves as a negative force within the home. Be gracious and loving in your relationships with the ones you love. Authority in the home is not the same as a power trip. Prayerfully consider your responses and decisions that affect your spouse and children. Be a team leader and they will follow you happily to the ends of the earth and into eternity.

'AMBITION' WORKSHEET

1. Do you see ambition as a positive or negative force in the following areas of life? Discuss your answers together.

Career?

Church?

Recreational activities?

Social encounters?

Your relationship with your spouse?

Your children?

Siblings and Parents?

2. Would your spouse and children call you honorable?

3. Would your spouse and children consider you famous in the things that matter?

20. AMEND

Sometimes when we marry we imagine we 'have arrived' when in reality we 'are beginning'. Many are under the false pretenses that the relationship is 'perfect as is', but will soon be introduced to the reality of the 'imperfect twosome'. That's where the "amending" idea comes in.

To grow better, together, changing, improving and to fill in the details of one's history is a necessary ingredient for success both as individuals and as a couple. Some of us are better at accepting change than others but we need to realize that relationships are continually adjusting, hopefully for the better but in some cases for the worse.

Try not to fight change. Life is evolving at a rapid rate of growth and we are all swept up in change daily. Our inner person is growing and maturing all through our lifetime and our character often determines the direction our outward advances make. Guard your character as you would a priceless gem. It is what people see and identify about you and it is your most precious legacy to leave your family. Everything you say and do hinges on noble character.

Also in the forefront of life, outside stimulant assault our thoughts, actions, dreams and goals demanding individual growth and improvement. This is good. They challenge us and present to us ambitions worthy of pursuit. It is life in motion and exciting.

But, since you are now married, any significant change that occurs in your individual life needs to be communicated with your spouse in order to avoid clashes, heartbreak and disappointments. Many a destructive wedge has been hammered in by well-meaning partners that refuse to respect and wait on their loved ones.

Be gentle and loving when introducing outward changes that will affect your partner. They may not be as eager or agreeable, needing additional time and encouragement to come on board with your ideas. They may even have opposing arguments to challenge you and help you to determine if there is a possible future in that direction. Be open to hear from your spouse and be humble enough to admit defeat should that become the case.

Improving and maturing in all aspects of life, whether it is inward character or outward circumstance, should be welcomed by all. Be sure to do all that you can do to challenge your partner to be everything that they were created to be and be willing to accept the same from them. Sometimes in communicating this to one another we fall into the 'negative' traps that ensnare and tear down relationships. Stay positive in your approach to these delicate issues and always have their heart-need at the forefront of any debate.

'AMEND' WORKSHEET

1. Were you under the false impression that life was perfect from day one and required no further tweaks?

2. Are you good at accepting change both internally and externally? Discuss.
How about personal change or those in your partner? Discuss.

3. How would you define your spouse's character? Discuss the positive and negative as it applies to your relationship as a couple or family.

4. Have you ever experienced insurmountable walls in your partner when trying to promote change?
Did you demand your way? How did you resolve the issue?
Are there borders you can set up to avoid conflict when approaching future changes?

5.Do you harbor any ill feelings or heartbreaks when recalling past encounters?

6. What is the one 'positive' ingredient to remember when dealing with change?

A

AMMUNITION

AMNESIA

AMUCK

AMUSEMENT

ANALYSIS

21. AMMUNITION

Ammunition comes in many forms. We usually think in terms of the military when we consider this word. In the armed forces bullets and missiles are meant for destruction; in the police force they arm themselves for self-defense and to uphold the law; as children they throw stones and punches to fight for their rights; as adults we use ambition, technology, words ... any good thing in a negative way to get our way.

Have you considered what destruction you can cause to a relationship with the wrong ammunition? You can quench someone's personal growth or dreams; you can speak words that kill both physically and emotionally; you can manipulate to get your own way; you can lie and cheat, steal and destroy. You have the ability to destroy the person who has willingly placed their life and wellbeing in your hands. You have the ability to produce scars in a trusting soul that are irremovable: When the two became one you gained the potential to ruin another life.

How can you do this? The majority of people do not set out to consciously ruin another human being, especially our spouse. We love our mates; that's why we married them. Somehow we manage to do it in bits and pieces, sometimes not even realizing the depth of hurt we are inflicting. Destructive ammunition in the marriage comes in many forms.

In your responses

In your priorities

In your selfish choices

In your unkind words and actions

In your trade offs

In your manipulative behavior

In your betrayal

In your lack of trust

In your self-centered motives

In your _____(you fill in the blank)

That's a peek at the destructive side.

Can we use ammunition positively? Of course we can. When a selfless character is dedicated to respecting and loving their spouse there are no limits to what this recipient can achieve both in their personal lives and in outward success.

We need to arm ourselves with ammunition that destroys the ills of our world and relationships, protects our way of life and serve to defend the ones we care about most, our families. Is there a positive way to use the above list of ammunition? In your responses, priorities, choices, words, actions, trust, motives, kindness, faithfulness, giving and loving.

Most of us do not fully consider how vulnerable we have become to our partners and how we sometimes allow them to trample on everything that is sacred and true to our character. Stay strong in your convictions, not with a demanding killer instinct, but gently persuading and living in the truth that you have at this present moment.

Your spouse should willingly respect and accept your individuality so that your character and worldview will not be destroyed. At the same time they expect the same consideration from you. Two individuals can live in harmony as long as both do not insist on singing the melody alone. Harmony comes with two voices of equal deliverance that serve to challenge and change their circle of influence for the better.

You chose to be a couple long ago on that wedding day. So stay united, gathering strength together as a couple, and use life's ammunition as a positive influence securing constructive results in the home and in our world. Arm yourselves with undefeatable ammunition.

'AMMUNITION' WORKSHEET

Please be kind with one another as you answer these questions.

1. Can you pinpoint any misuse of character ammunition in your relationship with your spouse?
In yourself? In your spouse?
Discuss with the goals of growing your relationship not killing it.

2. Can you pinpoint any external misuse of ammunition that you have demanded of your partner in the past?

3. Are there new boundaries that need to be defined and set up to protect one another?

Either from onslaughts that our partner never intended to inflict on us:
Or from misuse of ammunition that they are sorry for when brought to light in this discussion?

4. Do you hear a harmony in your relationship that:

Will strengthen you as a couple?

Will leave a witness and legacy for generations to come?

5. Are you both armed with positive ammunition to reach and witness to a needy world?

22. AMNESIA

Amnesia is not usually thought of in a positive way. It is often linked with heartbreak, illness and sadness in 'forgetting' things that should be remembered. We watch our loves ones withdraw and become alienated from us, breaking down communication between us, and causing a heartbreaking separation. Memory loss is a sad state to occupy, either as the victim or the loved one watching on.

In others cases we may consider it a blessing if we could somehow pull the switch on a particular memory that replays in our heads and laughs mockingly at our moments of stupidity and sin. Of course we can't. Only God can heal such memories. For His part, He erases our sin from his mind when we repent and ask Him for forgiveness; He has promised that our sins are as far as the east is from the west. For our part, we need to forgive ourselves and move on. That's a hard fix for ourselves but especially so for those who cause us pain.

Obviously I am not God and my mind is not nearly so kind and gracious as His. When my partner sins against me forgiveness and acceptance are much more difficult to achieve. So, is it possible and how do we do it?

Consider this scenario. Consciously or subconsciously your partner has either violated you emotionally, physically or in deed. The scene is playing rerun in your head and emotions are peeked and unable to reason. Wouldn't this be a great time to have memory loss? You hate the way you are feeling and the paths your thoughts are travelling. You genuinely desire for all the positive elements of your relationship to override the hurt and confusion, but truth evades you like a fleeting shadow and at this point you are fighting to stay in control of your mind and reactions.

Now is the time to stand firm on the foundation that you have built your marriage upon. Cling to the things you remember most to be true. You and your partner have built a history of battling the forces that would seek to destroy you as a couple. Take a deep breath, return to the house of memories that you have built together and allow healing to flow.

With unconditional love as your alibi, confront this new wall that has invaded your intimacy. Be brave and schedule a time in which to share your feelings, your twist on the violation, and your hope for reconciliation. Then wait for a response from your partner.

Hopefully communication and honesty will win out in the end. Two working together can overcome any obstacles that come against you as a couple. There is strength in the power of marriage. Finally when the relationship is healed, memory loss will take place in your heart. If the scene tries to torment you with ill-timed reruns, file the anguish in the 'trash department' of your mind and claim the victory you deserve in the active preservation of a well-established relationship.

So, in actual truth we will never experience total memory loss for the words said or the life led. They will attempt to drag us down and force us to live in the negative. But, I challenge you to plant your feet securely in the truth, walk in the healing and claim abundant life for you and your spouse. When you concentrate on the positive and press forward, then the memories you once wished you could forget will provide a stabilizing strength and a powerful testimony!

'AMNESIA' WORKSHEET

1. Have you had to deal with a loved one who is experiencing memory loss as a result of illness or accident?

Discuss your feelings and fears with your spouse.

2. Is there a memory that you continue to struggle with, one that has pushed a wedge between you and your spouse?

3. Can you claim victory to an experience with your spouse where you have worked through a trial and come out the other end together and stronger?

4. What ingredient would you add as a remedy for survival of a violation incurred by your spouse?

5. Is there someone in your circle of influence that you can help through a hurtful time who is on the brink of giving up?

23. AMUCK

Surviving in this world of fast living makes it extremely easy to run amuck in our own frantic frenzy. We are becoming experts in microwave living. Despite the advancement in technology that makes the tasks in our life so much easier, we still seem to not have enough hours in our day. Is social and technological advancement making us happier than the pioneers of olden days?

It's debatable! There are definitely positive contributions that have been integrated into our lives over the years. It becomes increasingly difficult to stay abreast of new breakthroughs because they change daily. When is enough, enough? Sometimes my head wants to scream *slow down: Smaller doses if you please! What's the rush?*

Yet the race continues and we are all caught up in it whether we realize it or not. Has it helped us to appreciate the simple things, the beauty of the world around us, the smells of a new day, the wonder of a child discovering something new for the first time? Does technology thrill the natural senses that crave first hand experience? Has any of it given you more time in your day to enjoy the blessings of life?

My biggest concern is the way in which the non-relational aspects of our lives consume us. The way meaningful connections to a real person are pushed aside to accommodate technology and the all-consuming race to the finish line. I suppose part of that is my generation talking, but nonetheless it disturbs me because marriage is a relationship that is on the chopping block. True intimacy is becoming a lost art for many couples and it feels easier to *go with the flow*. So marriages run amuck, as many people drown themselves in flippant and non-committal affairs, snuffing the life from their dying conscience and denying a high standard of morality.

When the strength of the marriage bond is gone society will also run amuck. When the next generation cannot see stable unconditional love in action they will become lost at a very early age and their adult contribution to society will be scarred and weak. Family is that important and its role in our society has eternal benefits that we can't even fathom.

Extra bonus: I have written a short essay, "Eroding Shadows": Thirteen Elements of Erosion for the Family Unit. It is available to you as a gift from Dream Creations when you subscribe to my website. http://marlenebierworth.com Hope to see you there.

'AMUCK' WORKSHEET

1. Do you feel overwhelmed in a world of frantic frenzy?

2. Can you think of ways you can salvage some time for the intimate things in your life and family?

3. Do you schedule dates with your spouse to keep the candle of love burning?

4. Do you have times in your home when technology is off limits and family activities take front stage?

5. Do you create social times to nurture the art of relationship with family and friends?

6. Do you rule technology in your home or does it rule you?

7. Do you spend too much time consumed in the business of life and forget to schedule the important relational adventures?

24. AMUSEMENT

Does your partner amuse you? Not in the condescending sense of word, but in an uplifting entertaining way that brings pleasure to your day.

Spontaneous surprises;

Jokes from out of nowhere;

Off-the-wall behavior with you probably being their biggest fan;

A character that you can delight and take pleasure in;

Someone who entertains, agreeably;

Someone you love to hang around just for the fun of it.

There is something very positive to be said about a sense of humor. It comes in many forms but the results are the same. They attract an audience: These are the people we love to hang around. We all need a good dose of laughter in our lives. Interaction with these folks often brings out the best in us, the mood becomes contagious and we discover that in hanging out with this person our whole attitude changes: our worries become fewer, stress levels goes into rest mode, and all the wonderful positive things about life become a magnet that draws us to the brighter side.

Wow, all that just because I am amused by something you said or did!

The bad news is that not all of us naturally come by this wonderful ability to lighten the mood in a room. There are many dimensions in this ability to amuse, from downright belly laughter to a faint smile that brings relief or a breath of fresh air to that moment. The very bad news is that some are so serious that they give off the opposite effect, creating sadness, boredom and gloom either in the room or in our spirit. We would all agree we do not want to camp there.

I have found in my natural, unchecked state, I lack the ability to cause contagious amusement in a room crowded with people. I tend to give off different vibes, positive ones but not necessarily hilarious ones. So, the question arises, is my partner lacking in the privilege of an amusing partner? No, in my case I am married to Mr.

Amusing himself and I unconsciously provide a check for him, a balance so to speak. But over time, I have found myself loosening up in that area and he actually finds me witty at times and there is no lack of smile on his face when he is with me. So we make a good team: fun and sensibility all wrapped up in the 'couple package'.

Have you thought about the role that amusement in any form plays in your life, whether it is just the two of you or you are one of many in a crowded room of people? I like to picture it as a positive injection into a serious world. I love to be amused whatever shape and form it takes in my day. It brings a healthy response and keeps our lives centered in the positive realm of existence.

Medically it is a natural cure for the mind, body, soul and spirit. People who thrive to live daily creating positive, happy moments are the very ones who will seek to squeeze every drop of this medicinal joy-juice into their being.

'AMUSEMENT' WORKSHEET

1. So, back to the introductory question: Does your partner amuse you?

2. Do you consider a sense of humor an important habit to encourage in your home or inside your circle of influence?

3. Discuss some humorous situations you can remember together as a couple. Did these occasions serve to bond you closer as a couple?

4. Can you think of a more serious aspect of your lives that could use an *attitude of amusement* injection? How so you think this will help you to cope in that particular mundane area of life?

5. From 1-10 how would you rate your ability to amuse people? Do you know how other people, especially your spouse views you in this area?

25. ANALYSIS

As a writer, analyzing is a huge part of my life. To take a fly-by idea from its initial scattered and unorganized form, then breaking it down into logical points of content, building themes, plots and synopsis and finally tackling each chapter and paragraph, winding all the way down to the nitty-gritty of sentence flow and arrangement discovering the perfect word that will resonate with the reader. All realizing that there is a hundred ways this same story could be presented and unique me has the privilege of selecting the right one. One way we practice this is tear another author's work apart, piece-by-piece, until it all makes sense.

Whew! That was a mouthful and not delivered in great sentence structure. I left the long sentences and wordy passage so that you would get an idea as to how involved the whole process of analysis is. My example will probably not be of major concern to your life but dissecting your life's data is a major concern, or it should be.

Hopefully as an engaged couple you shared your dreams, goals and visions in all areas of your life; home, children, God and church, careers, location, social interests. This introductory, getting-to-know-you phase, was simply a place to begin, for we all know that control over one's life has a way of slipping fast from our grasp.

As a couple we need to regroup and analyze what we are doing right and what went wrong since the last session. It is recommended that you do this often. Ask any businessperson how often the firm meets to develop new strategies and plans. They do it regularly. The next meeting is already scheduled before the present meeting adjourns.

A lot of couples I know have one big planning session in the New Year where life on every level of family existence is all hashed out and rewritten. Of course throughout the year there will be mini-meetings when unexpected things get thrown in the pathway. Be flexible! Don't stress change, but instead address it at the onset and resolve it to the best advantage for your family, and then move on.

Never compare your life's focus to any else around you, no matter how much you respect their ideals and success. Analyze your life, and your life alone. You are unique and your future is not to be held in the light of any else's expectations. As a family you have been staged in a specific place to create history, to move in the physical and spiritual realms of our society and church. There is no one like you as an individual and together much can be accomplished in a short life span. There is strength in the regrouping so decide today to take a positive step toward building the future that you were designed to walk in.

We have been granted the ability to have abundant life and success. Be sure to measure it carefully; not in the world's objective of chasing idols and temporary gain but in the light of eternity where the measuring stick has no limits to success.

'ANALYSIS' WORKSHEET

1. Does analysis (the breaking up of the bigger picture into smaller parts) scare you in any way?

2. Are you or your partner the stronger leader in this area?

Allow them to take the lead but never *settle* for any direction that the two of you have not agree upon, or at least agreed to disagree. This is a family corporation and all votes around the table are important for consideration before moving forward.

3. Did you and your fiancé plan your goals and dreams before the wedding? Have any evolved over the years?

4.Do you have a specific date on your calendar for a yearly planning session? Six month planning session?

5. Are you so set in stone that surprises mid-way throw you into panic? Discuss ways you can prepare yourself for the inevitable.

6. Can you recognize any definite U-turns in your lives that have changed your direction drastically? Were they positive or negative?
Is there anything you learned from the successes and failures of these seasons?

A

ANCHOR

ANGER

ANNIVERSARY

ANNUAL

ANTIDOTE

26. ANCHOR

We have all experienced the benefit of the anchor. The availability to ground yourself before a catastrophe; the availability to anchor down, stop and regroup; the strength of this solid instrument to hold our foundation secure while we go about our business.

Anchors can come in the form of inanimate objects: a house, career, bank account, school and church buildings, the anchor that holds a great ship at bay, any firmly fixed object that gives a measure of security.

Valuable anchors come in human form and can be counted as true gems worth more than all your gold. The next time you need to anchor in the midst of a life storm take note that you will not find solace in the material possessions that you have acquired. You will draw upon mankind, your human relationships that you have invested time and lots of unconditional love to build.

Hopefully the first person, other that Almighty God Himself that you will find on your list of anchors is your partner. They are the ones that vowed to stand by in, through all the storms of life. They can come alongside to shelter and encourage you, keep your feet firmly planted, hold the ship at bay while you struggle through the intricacies and emotions of the threatening waves.

It is our duty and privilege to love others through their storms. Empathy for the hurting is becoming a lost art. We have become so busy and self-focused that often we miss the signals of distress, carrying on as if life were normal. I pray to see people through the lens of God so that opportunities to encourage, pray and offer practical help will not slip me by.

It is often especially difficult to spot the small continuous pounding of the destructive waves beating on the people closest to us. Somehow we miss them, possibly from familiarity or maybe we take their presence for granted. Whatever the case the time will come when we will notice. We will wonder why suddenly they have alienated themselves and are acting in a peculiar manner. If the person affected is not quick to communicate with those she loves, walls are built between couples one stone at a time until the fortress of defense is not easily brought down.

'ANCHOR' WORKSHEET

1. Who is your number 1 anchor? Why?

2. Where is your spouse on the list of human anchors? Are there circumstances where another person would be more qualified to hold your partner up?

2. Have you considered God into the picture of anchoring your life and marriage?

3. Have you found yourself putting your faith in temporary things to keep you afloat in times of trouble?

4. Have you built relationships that you can count on to anchor you should the need arise?

5. Do you have the eyes to see the storms in people's lives that you cross paths with every day?

27. ANGER

Anger is such an explosive topic. Anyone who has lived with an angry person can relate to this. They seldom realize how often it happens and can usually justify their outbursts. Of course there are many levels of voicing and acting out anger from raising the voice to a destructive force that leaves victims in their wake both physically and emotionally.

A negative outburst of anger on any level is inexcusable. There are countless ways to handle the abrasive circumstances that cross our paths daily. As we mature we evaluate what works and what doesn't work in relationships with people. Hopefully we will learn to choose a response that is positive, healing and one that ends peacefully. After all it should not be our goal to have a physical fight, which strong, unbending words will eventually lead to.

Anger is seldom about the moment. It can have any number of sources:

Perhaps you have been met with obstacles and verbal abuse all day long and this is the last straw. Learn not to hide the hurt inside until it has nowhere else to go but burst the seams of your patience reserve. A slow fuse is just as deadly when it explodes.

Perhaps you regularly explode at the first offence and have never walked in the fruits of self-control. I have heard it said, "That's just the way I am. Like it or lump it!" If everyone said this, the world would be a scary place indeed: Individuals, claiming freedom to execute their own piece of damage to innocent victims simply because they have the right to be angry. It is just who I am. Poor pity that person. Yet, at the same time we realize there is an element in all of us that demonstrates poor and hurtful behavior to the people around us. None of us are exempt from sin but all of us can seek to grow and change our behavior so that our encounters are uplifting and profitable.

Perhaps you have triggers that are built in subconsciously and you don't even know how to control the outbursts. There are many in society that have grown up in delinquent homes, hearing and being the targets of abuse that results from anger. Unfortunately if it is not dealt with, these same victims grow to abuse their loved ones the same way. It is a circle of circumstance that needs to be broken.

Perhaps it is a chemical disorder that the angry person is at the mercy of, so in that case the problem needs to diagnosed and medicated so they can live a somewhat emotionally balanced life. This is probably the most frustrating of all because although it may be a chemical imbalance some of the time, it makes it difficult for the average onlooker to know when the angry person has crossed the line. There is a chance that they are simply being a rebellious person who carries the excuse of a medical condition and can get away with whatever they want. The caregiver needs to seek discernment daily and learn how to dish out tough love when necessary.

Perhaps you are sadistic and enjoy the power trip of watching people squirm under this abusive attack. All of us can feel intimidated by people of this nature. Anger of this magnitude is obvious in every syllable, action and threat. People of tact and wisdom can put these people in their place for the moment but become prey to the dark anger of the one seeking dominance. While others just crumble and become a victim over and over again. These are bullies in the worst form, for evil vengeance is at the heart of all they do. Sadly the bully usually comes from a background of being bullied and needs help to overcome their problem.

Perhaps you have read the bible, know the solution to the anger issue but choose not to walk the talk. Many people who believe that they are Christians refuse to let God into all of the dark recesses of their mind. The angry one can falsely justify his outbursts by his righteousness through Christ Jesus; *"This is wrong and I will deal with it, like it or not."* To them the line becomes fuzzy about whether this is God's judgment (which in truth we do not need to avenge) or their judgment; either way they are just as riled up. God requires only of us to stand firm and watch the power and glory of the Lord take up the battle. Responding in anger will never resolve an angry issue.

Perhaps you justify your anger because you know it all and expect the world to bow down to your way. "Doing it my way," is the way of the world. All ideas are acceptable whether they trample on everything the country has been built on or turn against the proven guidelines that God has revealed in the Word to protect us. Without right and wrong the people have no focus, no line drawn in which to clearly define the crossover. Anything goes, so the loudest, most offensive and obtrusive voice demands to win the day. This is the world we live in and we are reaping a sinful harvest of hybrid feasting.

In the preceding paragraphs I have outlined some of the anger issues that come to mind. I am certain that there are more excuses for anger that I did not touch on, and then even layered anger more deadly than the mind can conceive. Angry people have one thing in common; they all feel their rights have been stepped on and actively seek to get their own way.

In a marriage we have discovered there is no such reality as 'having our own way!' and the 'rights issue' was thrown out the window on day one. So in essence, anger has no place in a healthy relationship between married couples. It is an agent of destruction and will pound in a wedge so deep that you will be lucky to find your way back to the level ground. So beware and guard your heart and mind against an angry spirit.

'ANGER' WORKSHEET

1. Do you or your spouse have an anger problem? Are you in denial?

2. Can you recognize yourself or your spouse in any of the scenarios that were suggested in the text?

3. What do you think is the root cause of most anger?

4. As a couple do you know any angry people you can pray for or minister to?

5. Do you believe you can become angry by living with an angry partner? If yes, how do guard your heart?

28. ANNIVERSARY

After such a heavy last chapter I'd like to lighten the mood with a party. Anniversary party! A woman's day to bask in wonderful memories and a husband's day to be reminded, "You forgot again!" This is a common joke you hear everywhere but in all fairness to the men the statement is overstated and not the heart of the majority of men.

Some folks just love any reason to celebrate but if you are a married couple these days every new year is a victory worth commemorating. This year I am rejoicing in 44 years with the love of my youth and I do not tire of his company. That is probably a good thing as he is soon retiring fully and we will be together 24/7.

So, what's it like in your home in the days leading up to your wedding anniversary? Do you drop hints, leave catalogues out with gift items circled in red, and encourage the kids to remind their father of the special day approaching? I suppose the real question you should be asking yourself is, *'do I deserve to be rewarded for the effort I have put into this relationship this past year?'* Ouch!

Maybe your anniversary date is a good day to schedule a heart to heart discussion on the present condition of your relationship with your spouse. Check off last year's victories and commit once again to work harder on the failures. Add the new issues that have surfaced over the year. This could be a date to take stock of how far we've come!

Or not! Most of us don't want to spoil our special day with a chance for a possible disagreement. We all want the evening to be smothered in love and all things that glitter. I must intervene here because personally glitter is not my expectation of a successful evening. But I do know many who have high expectations and beware fellows not to plan a supercharged night that can never be topped. Next year is coming.

Many find that anniversary, birthdays; any celebration that marks a special day does make merit recognition on their 'happy list' of things to do. It's just not that important. Make sure that your spouse knows where your heart lies with regards to this delicate issue so that you will not be disappointed when he barely takes notice, or vise versa.

This is an opportunity to highlight the occasion for your spouse in a way that is unique and special to them. It could cost a fortune or be a totally free evening. Success is not weighed by the money spent but in the time of intimacy together. Plan carefully and rejoice in your victory and be grateful, for there are many marriages that did not survive the year.

'ANNIVERSARY' WORKSHEET

1. Do you have any special traditions that you observe on your wedding anniversary day?

2. Have you ever discussed how your spouse feels about celebrating yearly events? Are some more important than others?

3. Do you think more men or women forget their anniversary days?

4. In a previous chapter we discussed how New Years might be a good day to review your goals and direction. Do you have a day scheduled that you review relational goals and ensure that each partner is still on target and/or happy?

5. Keeping the lines of communication flowing will help to bring on another year of marital victory? Are you dedicated to continually exchanging ideas and feelings with one another?

HAVE A BLESSED ANNIVERSAY WHENEVER AND WHEREVER YOU CELEBRATE IT THIS YEAR!

29. ANNUAL

An annual event, celebrating something that has been completed in the course of a year, is a great way to mark advances and failures in the life of your marriage.

One of the ways you can accomplish this is by setting annual times to **evaluate the completion of a goal**.

1. It could be something as practical as assessing the childcare establishment that you chose to enroll your child.

2. It could be as emotional as a personal disappointment in your spouse.

3. It could be as spiritual as a major victory or set back in your walk with God.

4. It could be as exciting as a mental breakthrough, an opportunity to advance in some area of life.

5. It could be a physical review in the way you exercise alone, together and as a family.

6. It could be a financial issue as simple as the value of a gym or golf membership verses a new monetary direction.

'ANNUAL' WORKSHEET

1. Do you have annual events scheduled to discuss both failures and victories in your marriage and family life?

2. Do you have trouble discussing the failure of goals previously set?

3. Take one failure and see if you can find something positive in the experience and turn it around to inspire victory.

4.Take one victory and celebrate it. Plan an event together and applaud the good choices you made to get there.

5. Discuss plans to abolish, amend details, change focus or keep things as they are in the following areas:
- Relationship with spouse
- Relationship between family members
- Financial goals

- Career goals
- Spiritual goals
- Emotional well-being
- Mental well-being

30. ANTIDOTE

A remedy counteracting poison or evil

Poison comes in many forms. It can be a chemical substance that reacts with the body causing the one infected to suddenly develop serious health troubles. That definition is one that we can relate to in the physical sense; the cause and effect that we would normally link together; antidote as a cure for poison.

There are other kinds of poison that come against us that are just as deadly to our emotions, intellect and spiritual wellbeing. They are probably popping into your mind right now as you read.

The tongue can be deadly poisonous, spewing out evil in one moment and words of affection in the next. This causes a great confusion. It is a contradiction of character, good verses evil, and infects the message you send to the people you care about, especially your spouse. Be wise in your choice of words and in the manner in which you thrust them out into the world.

You never know who is listening and when you risk that someone's life will be forever marred by something you said in a careless moment.

False teaching can infect the way you think about everything. There are people who are experts in deception and without a discerning spirit you will fall victim and lose much in the lie.

Your **spiritual** life is at risk: Know the truth, walk in it, let it shine on the darkness around you and it will set you free.

Your **physical** life is at risk: Fads and diets, unrealistic physical achievements that border recklessness, busyness and abuse.

Your **mind** is at risk: People with a silver tongue that have the ability to sweet talk and convince you to believe anything.

Your **heart** is at risk: One-way relationships that demand everything from you but give nothing in return.

Your **joy** is at risk: Don't allow anyone to steal the joy of the Lord, for it is your strength for today and the days to come.

Your **finances** are at risk: remember we are only stewards of our fiancés so beware of those who can cheat you out of your life's savings. The Lord has blessed abundantly. Seek His direction.

Now that we have touched on some of the sources of poison and evil that can cross our paths, it is important to know that there is an antidote. His name is Jesus.

'ANTIDOTE' WORKHEET

1. What antidote do you have in place as a couple to counteract the poison that comes against your marriage?

The tongue...

False teaching...

Spiritual...

Physical...

Mind...

Heart...

Joy...

Finances...

Other?

2. Does the 'Jesus' antidote play as a remedy for the poison that attacks you as a couple?

ABOUT THE AUTHOR

MARLENE BIERWORTH has been married for 43 years to her husband, Paul. She is the mother of two children Jason and Pamela Five grandchildren complete her joy. Marlene is a published author.

I trust you have been challenged by sections 4
through 6 of The
A B C's of Marriage
Thank you for investing in your dream marriage!

Take your time and get a firm grasp on the topics covered in this SECOND book of 'Marriage Tips from the Alphabet'.

Be sure to watch for Book # 3 coming to Amazon. We will continue with the letter A and discover new challenges for discussion and growth in the lives of couples everywhere.

Please take the time to leave a book review on Amazon and let us know how the challenges helped or encouraged you in your daily walk through this wonderful event we call married life.

Also **let your friends and neighbors know**. Help them benefit from a time of study and reflection with the partner that they have chosen to spend the rest of their lives with.

I pray a blessing on your marriage and commitment to one another. I thank you for your willingness to step out and be challenged to be the best couple that you can possibly be!

JOIN ME

View all my book titles on my Amazon Author Page: http://www.amazon.com/-/e/B00J9RM116

Join me on social media and subscribe to my blog: http://marlenebierworth.com

Facebook: https://www.facebook.com/pages/Author-Marlene-Bierworth/481139081962391 *like my page

Twitter: https://twitter.com/MBierworth

OTHER BOOKS FROM MARLENE BIERWORTH

The Dream Series

1. Dreams With Feet

2. Sabotaged Dreams

The Secret Series

1. Family Secrets: The Novel (softcover)

2. Family Secrets (6 episodes in digital format of the 'Novel')

- o   A Premonition ...
- o   Betrayed ...
- o   Break Point ...
- o   Hate or Love ...
- o   Skeletons ...
- o   Bizarre: The final Book ...

Orphan Flower

1. Orphan Flower: The Novel

Short Stories

1. Revenge Backfired (Teen Romance)

2. A Fool's Rescue (Teen Romance)

Non-fiction Books

1. From "I Do" to "I Still Do"

2. The ABC'S of Marriage: Book 1

3. The ABC'S of Marriage: Book 2

Made in the USA
Monee, IL
14 November 2022

17715062R10052